# Zoom In on
# Desert Animals

# Camels

Leo Statts

**abdopublishing.com**

Published by Abdo Zoom™, PO Box 398166, Minneapolis, Minnesota 55439. Copyright © 2017 by Abdo Consulting Group, Inc. International copyrights reserved in all countries. No part of this book may be reproduced in any form without written permission from the publisher. Abdo Zoom™ is a trademark and logo of Abdo Consulting Group, Inc.

Printed in the United States of America, North Mankato, Minnesota
062016
092016

Cover Photo: iStockphoto
Interior Photos: Shutterstock Images, 1, 4–5, 10, 16; Anthon Jackson/Shutterstock Images, 6; iStockphoto, 7; Wolfgang Zwanzger/Shutterstock Images, 8–9; Odelia Cohen/iStockphoto, 9; Jan Miko/Shutterstock Images, 11; Denis Burdin/Shutterstock Images, 12–13; Red Line Editorial, 13, 20 (left), 20 (right), 21 (left), 21 (right); Robert Ford/iStockphoto, 15; Zambezi Shark/iStockphoto, 18–19

Editor: Brienna Rossiter
Series Designer: Madeline Berger
Art Direction: Dorothy Toth

**Publisher's Cataloging-in-Publication Data**
Names: Statts, Leo, author.
Title: Camels / by Leo Statts.
Description: Minneapolis, MN : Abdo Zoom, [2017] | Series: Desert animals |
    Includes bibliographical references and index.
Identifiers: LCCN 2016941124 | ISBN 9781680791785 (lib. bdg.) |
    ISBN 9781680793468 (ebook) | ISBN 9781680794359 (Read-to-me ebook)
Subjects: LCSH: Camels--Juvenile literature.
Classification: DDC 599.63--dc23
LC record available at http://lccn.loc.gov/2016941124

# Table of Contents

# Camels

Camels are **mammals**.
They have **humps**.

They can go many days
without food or water.

Arabian camels have one hump.

# Bactrian camels have two humps.

## Body

A camel has long legs.
It has a long, curved neck.

Its fur is thick.
This helps it stay cool.

# A camel has two rows of eyelashes.

They are long. They protect its
eyes from sand.

# Habitat

Camels live in Africa and Asia.
Some also live in Australia.

Where camels live

People train them to carry loads. Some Bactrian camels still live in the wild. They live in deserts.

# Food

Camels eat dry and thorny plants. They are ruminants. They can eat lots of food at once. It is stored in their humps as fat.

# Life Cycle

Camels have one
or two babies
at a time.

Calves
stay with their
mothers for one
to five years.
Camels can live
for 40 years in
the wild.

# Average Height

## At the shoulder an Arabian camel is shorter than a door.

6 ft 6 in                    6 ft 8 in

# Average Weight

An Arabian camel is as heavy as a soda vending machine.

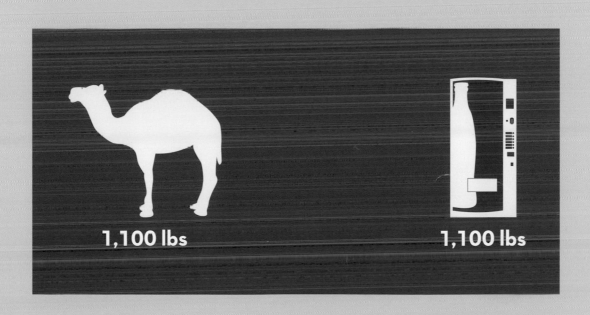

1,100 lbs

1,100 lbs

# Glossary

**calf** - a baby animal.

**desert** - a very dry, sandy area with little plant growth.

**hump** - a round bump on a camel's back that is made from fat.

**mammal** - an animal that makes milk to feed its young and usually has hair or fur.

**ruminant** - an animal that has more than one stomach and chews cud.

# Booklinks

For more information
on **camels**, please visit
booklinks.abdopublishing.com

## Zoom In on Animals!

Learn even more with the Abdo Zoom
Animals database. Check out
**abdozoom.com** for more information.

# Index